HBJ TREASURY OF LITERATURE

SLIVER OF THE MOON

SENIOR AUTHORS
ROGER C. FARR
DOROTHY S. STRICKLAND

AUTHORS
RICHARD F. ABRAHAMSON
ELLEN BOOTH CHURCH
BARBARA BOWEN COULTER
MARGARET A. GALLEGO
JUDITH L. IRVIN
KAREN KUTIPER
JUNKO YOKOTA LEWIS
DONNA M. OGLE
TIMOTHY SHANAHAN
PATRICIA SMITH

SENIOR CONSULTANTS
BERNICE E. CULLINAN
W. DORSEY HAMMOND
ASA G. HILLIARD III

CONSULTANTS
ALONZO A. CRIM
ROLANDO R. HINOJOSA-SMITH
LEE BENNETT HOPKINS
ROBERT J. STERNBERG

HARCOURT BRACE JOVANOVICH, INC.
Orlando   Austin   San Diego   Chicago   Dallas   New York

Printed in the United States of America

ISBN 0-15-301362-1

1 2 3 4 5 6 7 8 9 10   048   96   95   94   93   92

Acknowledgments
For permission to reprint copyrighted material, grateful acknowledgment is made to the following sources:
Bradbury Press, an Affiliate of Macmillan Publishing Company, Inc.: "The Snow Glory" from *Henry and Mudge in Puddle Trouble* by Cynthia Rylant, illustrated by Sucie Stevenson. Text copyright © 1987 by Cynthia Rylant; illustrations copyright © 1987 by Sucie Stevenson.
Dial Books for Young Readers, a division of Penguin Books USA Inc.: *Peace at Last* by Jill Murphy. Copyright © 1980 by Jill Murphy.
Aileen Fisher: "Dreams" from *Up the Windy Hill* by Aileen Fisher. Copyright renewed. Published by Abelard Press, New York, 1953.
Four Winds Press, an imprint of Macmillan Publishing Company: Cover illustration from *Emma's Lamb* by Kim Lewis. Copyright © 1991 by Kim Lewis.
Greenwillow Books, a division of William Morrow & Company, Inc.: Cover illustration from *The Quilt* by Ann Jonas. Copyright © 1984 by Ann Jonas. "I'm Awake, I'm Awake!" from *My Parents Think I'm Sleeping* by Jack Prelutsky. Text copyright © 1985 by Jack Prelutsky. Cover illustration by Nonny Hogrogian from *I Am Eyes: Ni Macho* by Leila Ward. Illustration copyright © 1978 by Nonny H. Kherdian.
Harcourt Brace Jovanovich, Inc.: Cover illustration from *Growing Vegetable Soup* by Lois Ehlert. Copyright © 1987 by Lois Ehlert.
HarperCollins Publishers: Cover illustration from *Who's Afraid of the Dark?* by Crosby Bonsall. Copyright © 1980 by Crosby Bonsall. "Tommy" from *Bronzeville Boys and Girls* by Gwendolyn Brooks. Text copyright © 1956 by Gwendolyn Brooks Blakely. Cover illustration by Garth Williams from *Bedtime for Frances* by Russell Hoban. Illustrations copyright © 1960 by Garth Williams. Cover illustration from *The Dream Factory* by Nurit Karlin. Copyright © 1988 by Nurit Karlin. Published by J. B. Lippincott. Illustration by Robin Spowart from "Oh Where, Oh Where Has My Little Dog Gone?" in *Songs from Mother Goose*, compiled by Nancy Larrick. Illustration copyright © 1989 by Robin Spowart. "Little Seeds" from *The Winds that Come from Far Away* by Else Holmelund Minarik. Text copyright © 1964 by Else Holmelund Minarik.
Houghton Mifflin Company: Jamaica's Find by Juanita Havill, illustrated by Anne Sibley O'Brien. Text copyright © 1986 by Juanita Havill; illustrations copyright © 1986 by Anne Sibley O'Brien.
Little, Brown and Company: Cover illustration from *Taking a Walk: A Book in Two Languages* by Rebecca Emberley. Copyright © 1990 by Rebecca Emberley. *Lost!* by David McPhail. Copyright © 1990 by David McPhail.
Macmillan Publishing Company: Dreams by Ezra Jack Keats. Copyright © 1974 by Ezra Jack Keats.
William Morrow & Company, Inc.: "Good Night" from *Vacation Time* by Nikki Giovanni. Text copyright © 1980 by Nikki Giovanni.
Partner Press: "Luna" from *Finger Frolics* compiled by Liz Cromwell, Dixie Hibner, and John R. Faitel. Text copyright © 1983 by Partner Press.
Picture Book Studio, Ltd.: Papa, Please Get the Moon for Me by Eric Carle. © 1986 by Eric Carle Corp.
Marian Reiner, on behalf of Eve Merriam: "Lights in the Dark" from *A Poem for a Pickle* by Eve Merriam. Text copyright © 1989 by Eve Merriam.
Elizabeth Roach: "Sleeping Outdoors" from *Rhymes About Us* by Marchette Chute. Text copyright 1974 by E. P. Dutton Co.
Simon & Schuster Books for Young Readers, New York: Cover illustration from *Happy Birthday, Moon* by Frank Asch. © 1982 by Frank Asch.
Seymour Simon: From *Silly Animal Jokes and Riddles* (Retitled: "Animals on the Move") by Seymour Simon. Text copyright © 1980 by Seymour Simon.
Tambourine Books, a division of William Morrow & Company, Inc.: Henny Penny by Stephen Butler. Copyright © 1991 by Stephen Butler.
Troll Associates, Mahwah, NJ: From *All About Seeds* by Susan Kuchalla. Text copyright © 1982 by Troll Associates. From *Stars* by Roy Wandelmaier, illustrated by Irene Trivas. Copyright © 1985 by Troll Associates.
John Wallner: Cover illustration by John Wallner from *Little Fox Goes to the End of the World* by Ann Tompert. Illustration copyright © 1976 by John Wallner.
Rose Wyler: From *What Happens If . . .?: Science Experiments You Can Do By Yourself* (Retitled: "Shadow Pictures") by Rose Wyler. Text copyright © by Rose Wyler.

Handwriting models in this program have been used with permission of the publisher, Zaner-Bloser, Inc., Columbus, OH.

Dear Reader,

Reading can make you feel like reaching for the stars. It can help you hold your very own sliver of the moon. In this book you will meet a young girl who does just that. You will also meet Roberto, a boy who saves a cat. See what happens when a bear gets lost in the city or when Jamaica finds a toy dog. Meet people from many different places. All have something wonderful to share.

Ready, set, turn the page. Stretch as far as you can!

Sincerely,
The Authors

CONTENTS

6

"Girls and boys, come out to play,
The moon is shining bright as day."
Mother Goose

Come out and enjoy the night!
What do you dream about at night? Wait
until you see the wood carvings that the
artists of Mexico dreamed up! As you
read these nighttime stories, think of all
the wonderful things you can see in the
night.

9

BOOKSHELF

THE QUILT
BY ANN JONAS

A young girl has a new quilt. Her mother and father made it for her from such things as her old baby pajamas and her first curtains. The first time she sleeps under it, she has an exciting dream!

HBJ LIBRARY BOOK

WHO'S AFRAID OF THE DARK?
BY CROSBY BONSALL

"Stella is afraid of the dark," a boy tells his friend. Who is Stella? How does the boy help her?

CHILDREN'S CHOICE

THE DREAM FACTORY
BY NURIT KARLIN

Baa Baa doesn't like to go to sleep. So Grandma takes her on a trip to the Dream Factory. Where is the Dream Factory? What goes on there?

HAPPY BIRTHDAY, MOON
BY FRANK ASCH

Bear wants to give the moon a birthday present. What special present can Bear give to the moon? CHILDREN'S CHOICE

BEDTIME FOR FRANCES
BY RUSSELL HOBAN

Frances is in bed at last after a glass of milk, a piggyback ride, and lots of good-night kisses. But she still can't sleep! She begins to think that all kinds of things are in her room.

ALA NOTABLE BOOK

11

In the house Baby Bear was
fast asleep, and Mrs. Bear had
turned over and wasn't snoring
anymore.
Mr. Bear got into bed and closed his
eyes.
"Peace at last," he said to h

PEACE AT LAST

by Jill Murphy

The hour was late.
Mr. Bear was tired, Mrs. Bear
was tired, and Baby Bear was tired,
so they all went to bed.

Mrs. Bear fell asleep.

Mr. Bear didn't.

Mrs. Bear began to snore.

"SNORE," went Mrs. Bear.

"SNORE, SNORE, SNORE."

"Oh, NO!" said Mr. Bear,

"I can't stand THIS."

So he got up and went to

sleep in Baby Bear's room.

Baby Bear was not asleep either.

He was lying in bed, pretending

to be an airplane.

"NYAAOW!" went Baby Bear.

"NYAAOW! NYAAOW!"

"Oh, NO!" said Mr. Bear,

"I can't stand THIS."

So he got up

and went to sleep in the living room.

TICK-TOCK . . . went the living room
clock. . . . TICK-TOCK, TICK-TOCK,
CUCKOO! CUCKOO!
"Oh, NO!" said Mr. Bear,
"I can't stand THIS."
So he went off to sleep in the kitchen.

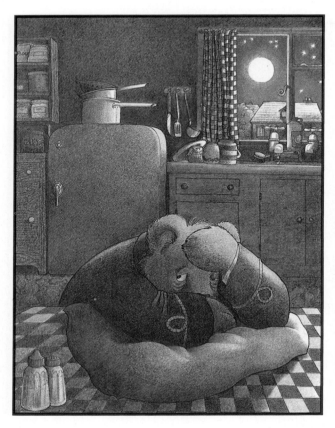

DRIP, DRIP . . . went the leaky

kitchen faucet.

HMMMMMMMMMM . . .

went the refrigerator.

"Oh, NO," said Mr. Bear,

"I can't stand THIS."

So he got up

and went to sleep in the garden.

Well, you would not believe what noises
there are in the garden at night.
"TOO-WHIT-TOO-WHOO!"
went the owl.
"SNUFFLE, SNUFFLE," went
the hedgehog.
"MIAAAOW!" sang the cats on the wall.
"Oh, NO!" said Mr. Bear,
"I can't stand THIS."
So he went off to sleep in the car.

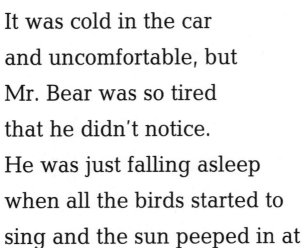

It was cold in the car
and uncomfortable, but
Mr. Bear was so tired
that he didn't notice.
He was just falling asleep
when all the birds started to
sing and the sun peeped in at
the window.
"TWEET TWEET!" went the birds.
SHINE, SHINE . . . went the sun.
"Oh, NO!" said Mr. Bear,
"I can't stand THIS."
So he got up and went back
into the house.

20

In the house Baby Bear was
fast asleep, and Mrs. Bear had
turned over and wasn't snoring
anymore.
Mr. Bear got into bed and closed
his eyes.
"Peace at last," he said to himself.

BRRRRRRRRRRRRRRR . . . went the
alarm clock. BRRRRRR!
Mrs. Bear sat up and rubbed her eyes.
"Good morning, dear," she said.
"Did you sleep well?"
"Not VERY well, dear," yawned Mr. Bear.
"Never mind," said Mrs. Bear. "I'll
bring you the mail and a nice cup of tea."

23

And she did.

THINK IT OVER

1. How did Mr. Bear find "peace at last"?

2. What else could Mr. Bear have done to get some sleep?

WRITE

What do you think Baby Bear would do if he could not fall asleep? Write some of your ideas.

25

I'M AWAKE! I'M AWAKE!
by Jack Prelutsky

I'm awake! I'm awake!
I cannot shut my eyes,
I'm unable to sleep,
though I've made many tries,

I'm sure I've explored
every inch of my bed,
my body's exhausted,
and so is my head.

I wiggle, I fidget,
I tumble, I twist,
I pound my poor pillow
with fist after fist,

I stopped counting sheep
when I reached ninety-three.
I'm awake! I'm awake!
I cannot fall asleeeeeeeeeeeeeee

illustrated by Vicki Wehrman

DREAMS
by Aileen Fisher

Do you ever
wonder too
what dreams do
when they
are through?

LIGHTS IN THE DARK
by Eve Merriam

In the quiet
of the night,
shining,
shining,
shining bright.

Emerald stars
or fireflies?

Cat's eyes,
cat's eyes,
cat's eyes.

GOOD NIGHT
by Nikki Giovanni

Goodnight Mommy
Goodnight Dad

I kiss them as I go

Goodnight Teddy
Goodnight Spot

The moonbeams call me so

I climb the stairs
Go down the hall
And walk into my room

My day of play is ending
But my night of sleep's in bloom

Jack Prelutsky's silly rhyming poems about people and animals have been making people laugh for years. He has worked as a taxi driver, bookseller, waiter, carpenter, and moving man. Jack Prelutsky often visits schools. There he reads his poems for children, plays the guitar, and sings.

Aileen Fisher grew up on a farm. As a child she liked to take long walks in the woods. There she learned to love animals and the outdoors. Her poems make us wonder about nature and everyday things.

Eve Merriam's poems are about things children like. Her poetry seems to ask the reader to join in the fun! Some of her poems are about bugs, animals, stars, and wishes.

Nikki Giovanni writes poems about people for children and adults. She writes about feelings children have, such as happiness and sadness. Some of her poems are about happy times she had as a child. Nikki Giovanni hopes that her poems will help people to better understand one another.

Dreams

CHILDREN'S
CHOICE

EZRA JACK KEATS

It was hot.
After supper Roberto came
to his window to talk with Amy.
"Look what I made in school today—
a paper mouse!"
"Does it do anything?" Amy asked.
Roberto thought for a while.
"I don't know," he said. Then he put
the mouse on the window sill.

33

As it grew darker, the city got quieter.

"Bedtime, Roberto," called his mother.

"Bedtime for you, too,"
other mothers called.

"Good-night, Amy."

"Good-night, Roberto."

"G-o-o-o-o-d-night!" echoed the parrot.

Soon they were all in bed.

Someone began to dream.
Soon everybody was dreaming—
except one person.
Somehow Roberto just couldn't
fall asleep. It got later and later.

37

Finally he got up
and went to the window.
What he saw down in the street
made him gasp!
There was Archie's cat!
A big dog had chased him into a box.
The dog snarled.
"He's trapped!" thought Roberto.
"What should I do?"

Then it happened!
His pajama sleeve
brushed the paper mouse
off the window sill.
It sailed away from him.

40

Down it fell,
turning this way
and that, casting a big shadow
on the wall.
The shadow grew bigger—
and bigger—

and BIGGER!
The dog howled and ran away.
The cat dashed across the street
and jumped through Archie's open window.
"Wow! Wait till I tell Archie what
happened!" thought Roberto.
"That was some mouse!"
He yawned and went back to bed.

Morning came, and everybody
was getting up.
Except one person.
Roberto was fast asleep,
dreaming.

Think It Over

1. Why do you think it was good that Roberto
   could not sleep?

2. How did Roberto save Archie's cat?

Write

Do you think Roberto will tell his friends about
what happened at night? Write what he might say.

What happened when Roberto's paper mouse fell out the window? That's right! The mouse's shadow could be seen on the wall. You can make shadows, too.

SHADOW

by Rose Wyler
illustrated by Jackie Snider

Put a flashlight on a table. Hold your hand in front of the light. Now walk to the wall. What happens to the shadow? Does it stay the same size?

At first the shadow is big. Your hand is near the flashlight and blocks a lot of light.

PICTURES

from WHAT HAPPENS IF . . . ?

As you walk to the wall, your hand blocks less and less light. The shadow gets smaller and smaller. When your hand is near the wall, the shadow is smallest of all.

Now make some shadow pictures. To make a duck, hold your hand this way. Make your fingers go up and down. The duck will talk.

Try making some other shadow pictures like this.

rabbit

cat

bird

horse

Can you make up a story about these shadow pictures?
Ask your friends to help you. Then put on a shadow show.

I CAN'T SLEEP

How are Mr. Bear and Roberto alike?

· ·

Who do you think feels happier in the morning, Mr. Bear or Roberto? What makes you think that?

· ·

WRITER'S WORKSHOP Write a poem about sleeping. Use some "sleepy" words. Draw a picture of your poem.

STARRY NIGHT

What do you know about stars?
Have you ever slept under the
stars? You can read and learn
about the stars!

CONTENTS

S·T·A·R·S

by Roy Wandelmaier
illustrated by Irene Trivas

Let's take a trip to the stars.

A star glows hot. A star glows bright.
Are all stars as hot as our sun? Some are even hotter!

The hottest stars give off blue light.
Cooler stars give off red light.

Our star, the sun,
is not the hottest or the coolest star.

It is in the middle.

It shines yellow.

After some stars live a long time,
they explode. We call this a supernova.

The exploded gas goes out into space.
And some of it may be used to make a new star.

Stars are so far away.

But stars are close enough to shine for us.

Watch for them tonight.

THINK IT OVER

1. What do you now know about stars?

2. Why do stars give off blue, yellow, or red light?

WRITE

Make believe you take a trip to the stars. Write about what you see.

SLEEPING OUTDOORS

by Marchette Chute

illustrated by Kathy Lengyel

Under the dark is a star,
Under the star is a tree,
Under the tree is a blanket,
And under the blanket is me.

STARRY NIGHT

What did you learn about red and yellow stars?

. . . .

If you were sleeping outdoors on a starry night, what would you do?

. . . .

WRITER'S WORKSHOP Draw a picture. Show yourself doing something outside in the starry night. Write a story about your picture.

63

LET'S GO TO THE MOON

Does the moon always look the same? What is the moon like? You can go to the moon with a story and a poem.

C O N T E N T S

CHILDREN'S CHOICE

Eric Carle PAPA, PLEASE GET THE MOON FOR ME

Papa, please get
the moon for me

ERIC CARLE

Before Monica went to bed she looked out
of her window and saw the moon.
The moon looked so near.

"I wish I could play with the moon," thought
Monica, and reached for it.

But no matter how much she stretched, she
could not touch the moon.

"Papa," said Monica to
her father, "please get
the moon for me."

Papa got a <u>very</u> long
ladder.

He carried the very long
ladder towards a <u>very</u> high
mountain.

Then Papa put the very
long ladder on top of the
very high mountain.

Up and up and up he climbed.

Finally, Papa got to the moon.

"My daughter Monica would like to play with you," said Papa, "but you are much too big."

"Every night I get a little smaller," said the moon.

"When I am just the right size you can take me with you."

And, indeed, the moon got smaller and smaller and smaller.

When the moon was just the right size, Papa took it. Down and down and down he climbed.

"Here," said Papa to Monica, "I have the moon for you."

Monica jumped and danced with the moon.

She hugged the moon and threw it into the air.

But the moon kept getting smaller and
smaller and smaller, and finally it
disappeared altogether.

Then, one night, Monica saw a thin sliver of the moon reappear.

Each night the moon grew . . .

and grew and grew.

THINK IT OVER

1. Why is <u>Papa, Please Get the Moon for Me</u> the name of the story?

2. How do you know that this story could not really happen?

WRITE

What is something you asked for and got? Write what you did with it.

L U N A

 As Earth's moon travels
on its way

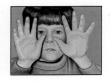 It's seen by night

 as well as day.

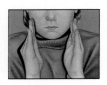 The first day it's skinny,

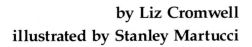 fourteenth it's round;

 Two weeks later
it can't be found.

by Liz Cromwell
illustrated by Stanley Martucci

LET'S GO TO THE MOON

What could you tell Monica about the moon?

. . . .

When would Papa not be able to get Monica the moon?

. . . .

WRITER'S WORKSHOP Pretend that you got the moon. When did you get it? What did it look like? What did you do with it? Draw a picture of what you would do. Write a story about your picture.

MULTICULTURAL CONNECTION

ARTISTS OF MEXICO

What do you dream about at night? Have you ever dreamed about animals like the ones in these pictures?

Artists get ideas from nighttime dreams and from daydreams, too. Artists in Mexico make these wonderful figures. They cut them out of wood first. Then they paint them bright colors. Colorful figures like these can be found in many museums.

■ Draw your own dream animal. Paint it many colors.

ARTISTS

There are many different kinds of artists in the world. Go to the library. Find a book about artists from other countries. Bring the book to class, and share what you learn.

NIGHTTIME ANIMALS

Many animals sleep during the day and come out at night. Name some of these animals. Draw a picture of one, and tell what it does at night.

UNIT TWO

ON·OUR·WAY

Where do you like to go? What do you like to see on your way? What would you like to be when you grow up? Jo Ann Jeong dreamed of being a park ranger and made her dream come true. As you read these stories, think about the dreams that might come true for you along your way.

THEMES

SIGNS OF SPRING

SILLY JOURNEYS

LOST AND FOUND

GROWING VEGETABLE SOUP
BY LOIS EHLERT

How can you grow your own vegetable soup? This book tells step by step how to grow yummy vegetable soup. It may take a while, but you can do it! AWARD-WINNING AUTHOR

HBJ LIBRARY BOOK

LITTLE FOX GOES TO THE END OF THE WORLD
BY ANN TOMPERT

Little Fox tells her mother that she wants to travel to the end of the world. She will fight the weather and many other things. What do you think she will see on her trip? ALA NOTABLE BOOK

EMMA'S LAMB
BY KIM LEWIS

Emma's father finds a lost lamb. Emma wants to keep the lamb as a pet. How will she care for the lamb? Will the lamb like its new home?

TAKING A WALK · *CAMINANDO*
BY REBECCA EMBERLEY

How do you say *balloon* in Spanish? How do you say *playground* in Spanish? Learn these words and more by taking a walk through this colorful book.

I AM EYES · *NI MACHO*
BY LEILA WARD

Find out what the words *Ni Macho* mean. Travel to a beautiful land, and look through the eyes of a young boy. See all the wonderful things he sees.

83

SIGNS OF SPRING

Do you like spring? Here are some stories and poems about things that grow in spring.

CONTENTS

85

The Snow Glory

by Cynthia Rylant

pictures by Suçie Stevenson

from **HENRY AND MUDGE IN PUDDLE TROUBLE**

When the snow melted and Spring came,
Henry and his big dog Mudge stayed
outside all the time.

Henry had missed riding his bike.
Mudge had missed chewing on sticks.
They were glad it was warmer.

87

One day when Henry and Mudge were
in their yard, Henry saw something blue
on the ground.

He got closer to it.

"Mudge!" he called. "It's a flower!"

Mudge slowly walked over and sniffed
the blue flower.

Then he sneezed all over Henry.

"Aw, Mudge," Henry said.

Later, Henry's mother told him that the flower was called a snow glory.

"Can I pick it?" Henry asked.

"Oh, no," said his mother. "Let it grow."

So Henry didn't pick it.

Every day he saw the snow glory in the yard, blue and looking so pretty.

He knew he shouldn't pick it.

He was trying not to pick it.

But he thought how nice it would look in a jar.

He thought how nice to bring it inside.

He thought how nice it would be to own that snow glory.

Every day he stood with Mudge and looked at the flower.

Mudge would stick his nose into the grass all around the snow glory.

But he never looked at it the way Henry did.

"Don't you think the snow glory has been growing long enough?" Henry would ask his mother.

"Let it grow, Henry," she would say.

Oh, Henry wanted that snow glory.

And one day he just knew he had to have it.

So he took Mudge by the collar and he stood beside the snow glory.

"I'm going to pick it," Henry whispered to Mudge.

"I've let it grow a long time."

Henry bent his head and he said in Mudge's ear, "Now I *need* it."

And Mudge wagged his tail, licked Henry's face, then put his big mouth right over that snow glory . . .

and he ate it.

"*No, Mudge!*" Henry said.

But too late.

There was a blue flower in Mudge's belly.

"I said *need* it, not *eat* it!" shouted Henry.

94

He was so mad because Mudge took his
flower.

It was Henry's flower and Mudge took it.

And Henry almost said, "Bad dog," but
he stopped.

He looked at Mudge, who looked back at
him with soft brown eyes and a flower in
his belly.

Henry knew it wasn't his snow glory.

He knew it wasn't anybody's snow glory.

Just a thing to let grow.

And if someone ate it, it was just a thing
to let go.

Henry stopped feeling mad.

He put his arms around Mudge's big
head.

"Next time, Mudge," he said, "try to
listen better."

Mudge wagged his tail and licked
his lips.

96

One blue petal fell from his mouth into Henry's hand.

Henry smiled, put it in his pocket, and they went inside.

THINK IT OVER

1. Why didn't Henry stay mad at Mudge?

2. How did you know that Mudge did not care much about the snow glory?

WRITE

What do you like to do in the Spring? Write about something else Mudge and Henry could do in the Spring.

TOMMY

I put a seed into the ground
And said, "I'll watch it grow."
I watered it and cared for it
As well as I could know.

One day I walked in my back yard,
And oh, what did I see!
My seed had popped itself right out,
Without consulting me.

by Gwendolyn Brooks

#

Little seeds we sow in spring,
growing while the robins sing,
give us carrots, peas and beans,
tomatoes, pumpkins, squash and greens.

And we pick them,
one and all,
through the summer,
through the fall.

Winter comes, then spring, and then
little seeds we sow again.

by Else Holmelund Minarik
illustrated by Tracy Sabin

All About Seeds

by Susan Kuchalla

What is a seed?
An acorn is a seed. A pine
cone holds seeds. A seed
can be a pit or a nut or
a bean.

Do you know what grows from a seed?
Plants grow from seeds. A flower is a
plant. A bush is a plant, and
so is a tree.

Do you know how seeds are planted?
Sometimes they just fall to the ground.
Sometimes they are carried and planted
by the wind.

Sometimes they are carried and planted
by water. Sometimes they are planted
by animals. And sometimes they are
planted by people.

Seeds need water to grow. Rain gives
them water. Or people can bring
water to them.

Seeds also need air and sunshine. The sun warms
the ground. The seed starts to grow. There is a
little plant in the seed. It grows and grows. Soon
the stem pushes up, and leaves grow.
Leaves reach out for sunlight. Plants make their
own food. The plant grows bigger and stronger.

What kind of plant will it be?

It might be a flower. It might be
a fruit or a vegetable. It might be
a pine tree. It might be a tree
that is covered with fruit.

But this plant grew from an acorn . . .

. . . so it will grow into a mighty oak tree!

THINK IT OVER

1. How does a seed grow?

2. What kind of seed would you like to plant? How would you care for it?

WRITE

Imagine that you must teach a friend how to grow a plant. Write five things you would tell your friend to do.

SIGNS OF SPRING

How do you think the snow glory grew?

. . . .

What would Henry want to tell Tommy about the seed that popped out?

. . . .

WRITER'S WORKSHOP Draw a picture of some signs of spring. Write about your picture. Tell some things about spring.

SILLY JOURNEYS

What's so funny? Read about some silly animals and the silly trips they take!

CONTENTS

HENNY PENNY

adapted from a retelling by Stephen Butler

Characters

Narrator   Cocky Locky   Goosey Loosey

Henny Penny   Ducky Lucky   Turkey Lurkey

Foxy Loxy

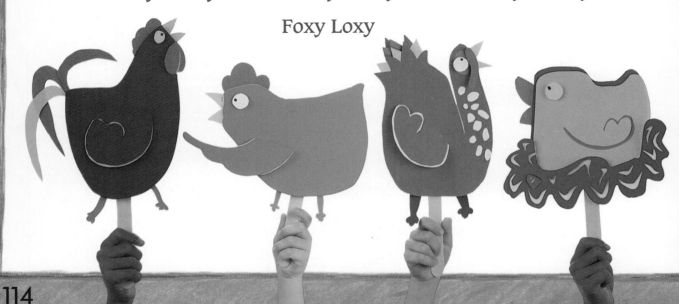

Narrator: One day while Henny Penny was sitting beneath the oak tree an acorn fell and hit her on the head.

Henny Penny: Goodness me! The sky is falling! I must go and tell the king.

Narrator: So Henny Penny ran off in a great hurry to tell the king the sky was falling. She had not gone far before she met Cocky Locky.

Cocky Locky: Where are you going,
Henny Penny?

Henny Penny: Oh, Cocky Locky! The sky is
falling! And I am going to tell the king.

Cocky Locky: Goodness me! I'll come with you.

Narrator: So Henny Penny and Cocky Locky
hurried on to tell the king the sky was falling.
They had not gone far before they met
Ducky Lucky.

Ducky Lucky: Where are you two going?

Cocky Locky: Oh, Ducky Lucky! The sky is falling! And we are going to tell the king.

Ducky Lucky: Goodness me! I'll come with you.

Narrator: So Henny Penny, Cocky Locky, and Ducky Lucky hurried on to tell the king the sky was falling. They had not gone far before they met Goosey Loosey.

Goosey Loosey: Where are you all going?

Ducky Lucky: Oh, Goosey Loosey! The sky is falling! And we are going to tell the king.

Goosey Loosey: Goodness me! I'll come with you.

Narrator: So Henny Penny, Cocky Locky, Ducky Lucky, and Goosey Loosey hurried on to tell the king the sky was falling. They had not gone far before they met Turkey Lurkey.

Turkey Lurkey: Where are you all going?

Goosey Loosey: Oh, Turkey Lurkey! The sky is falling! And we are going to tell the king.

Turkey Lurkey: Goodness me! I'll come with you.

Narrator: So Henny Penny, Cocky Locky, Ducky Lucky, Goosey Loosey, and Turkey Lurkey hurried on to tell the king the sky was falling. Suddenly Foxy Loxy appeared.

Foxy Loxy: And where are you all going in such a hurry?

All Birds: Oh, Foxy Loxy! The sky is falling! We are going to tell the king.

Foxy Loxy: But you're going the wrong way! The king's palace is that way.

Narrator: Foxy Loxy pointed to a path leading into the woods. So Henny Penny, Cocky Locky, Ducky Lucky, Goosey Loosey, and Turkey Lurkey hurried down the path. They ran on and on until at last they reached the king's palace.

Foxy Loxy: Come in and tell me your story, Henny Penny.

Narrator: But as Henny Penny curtsied, she saw a bushy red tail beneath the king's robe.

Henny Penny: It's a trap! Run!

Narrator: Foxy Loxy threw off his cunning disguise and sprang to the door.

Foxy Loxy: Surprise! I'm going to eat you all for dinner.

Narrator: Henny Penny woke up with a start and opened her eyes. She was still trembling.

Henny Penny: Goodness me! I must have been dreaming.

Narrator: But just then an acorn fell and hit her on the head.

Henny Penny: Goodness me! The sky is falling! I must go and tell the king.

THINK IT OVER

1. Why were Henny Penny and her friends going to see the king?

2. How did you know that the story was just Henny Penny's dream?

WRITE

Imagine that you are Ducky Lucky. You want to tell Henny Penny that the sky is not really falling. Write what you would say.

Animals on the Move

from <u>Silly Animal Jokes and Riddles</u>
written by Seymour Simon
illustrated by Susan Swan

"What are you doing, Junior?" asked Mother Lion.

"I'm chasing a hunter around his car," answered Junior Lion.

"How many times have I told you not to play with your food?"

HA HA HA

Teacher: Can a duck fly upside-down?

Student: No. It would quack up.

Sunny Beach
100 Miles

Teacher: Why do wild geese fly south in the fall?

Student: Because it's too far to walk.

SILLY JOURNEYS

Why was Henny Penny's trip to see the king silly?

· ·

Which do you think is funnier, "Henny Penny" or one of the jokes? Why?

· ·

WRITER'S WORKSHOP Pretend you are Henny Penny. Write a letter about your silly journey to an animal from "Animals on the Move."

129

THEME

LOST AND FOUND

Have you ever found something? What was it? Read to see what is "Lost and Found"!

CONTENTS

131

I am walking down the street when I hear
someone crying.

It's a bear!

He looks lost and afraid.

The tall buildings scare him.

And he's never seen so many people.

"Don't worry," I tell him.

"The buildings won't hurt you, and

most of the people are friendly.

How did you get here?" I ask.

"I climbed in to have a nap,"

he explains, "and when I woke up,

I was *lost!*"

"I'll help you. Tell me where you live."

"There are trees where I live," he tells me.

So we find some trees.

"More trees," he says, "and water!"

I take him to a place where there are more
trees—and water, too.

"No," he says. "This is not it either."

I have an idea. "Follow me!" I say.

137

I take him to a tall building.

We go inside, get on the elevator, and ride all
the way to the top.

From up here we can see the whole city.

"Look!" I say. "Now we can find your home."

"There it is!" he says, pointing.

Down we go, across three streets
and into the park.
The park is not the bear's home
after all—but he likes it there.
We go for a boat ride,
we have lunch,
and we go to the playground.
We are having a good time.

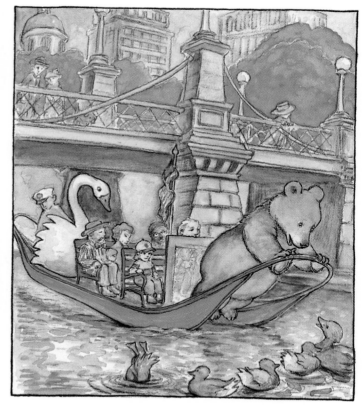

But it is getting late, and the bear is still lost.

"Let's try the library," I tell him.

"We can find out anything here!"

Inside the library we look through lots of books.

The bear sees a picture that looks like his home.

We find the place on a map and hurry outside.

A bus is leaving.

We get on the bus and ride for a long time.

Finally, we are there.

"*This* is where I live!" says the bear.

He gives me a hug and thanks me again
for my help.

Then he waves good-bye and disappears
into the forest.

The trees are so tall, and there aren't any people.

"Wait!" I call to the bear, "come back!

I think I'm lost!" I tell him.

"Don't worry," he says. "I will help you."

THINK IT OVER

1. How did the bear and the boy help each other?

2. How would you help a lost animal?

WRITE

How will the bear help the boy find his home? Write a new ending to the story.

Words About the Author and Illustrator:

David McPhail

David McPhail writes the words and draws the pictures for his books. He began to draw when he was two years old. He has been drawing beautiful pictures ever since.

Mr. McPhail sometimes writes about animals who act just like children. The bear in "Lost!" talks and feels just as you might feel if you were lost. Would you like to read more about a bear and a boy? Read <u>The Bear's Toothache</u> and <u>First Flight</u> by David McPhail.

Oh Where, Oh Where Has My Little Dog Gone?

Oh where, oh where has my little dog gone?
Oh where, oh where can he be?
With his ears cut short and his tail cut long,
Oh where, oh where is he?

illustrated by Robin Spowart

Jamaica's Find

Juanita Havill

Illustrations by Anne Sibley O'Brien

When Jamaica arrived at the park, there was no one there.

It was almost supper time, but she still had a few minutes to play.

She sat in a swing, pushed off with her toes, and began pumping.

It was fun not to have to watch out for the little ones who always ran in front of the swings.

151

Then she climbed up the slide.

There was a red sock hat on the ladder step.

Jamaica took it for a ride.

She slid down so fast that she fell in the sand and lay flat on her back.

When she rolled over to get up, she saw a stuffed dog beside her.

It was a cuddly gray dog, worn from hugging.

All over it were faded food and grass stains.

Its button nose must have fallen off.

There was a round white spot in its place.

Two black ears hung from its head.

Jamaica put the dog in her bicycle basket.

She took the hat into the park house and gave it to the young man at the counter.

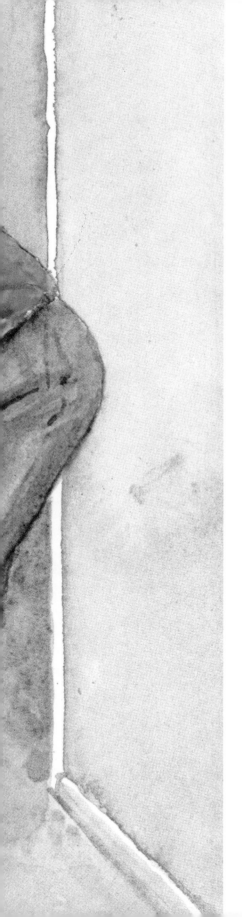

The first thing her mother said when Jamaica came in the door was: "Where did that dog come from?"

"The park. I stopped to play on the way home," Jamaica said.

"I found someone's red hat and took it to the Lost and Found."

"But, Jamaica, you should have returned the dog, too," said her mother.

Then she said, "I'm glad you returned the hat."

"It didn't fit me," Jamaica said.

"Maybe the dog doesn't fit you either," her mother said.

"I like the dog," said Jamaica.

"Don't put that silly dog on the table!"
Jamaica's brother said.

"You don't know where it came from.
It isn't very clean, you know," her father
said.

"Not in the kitchen, Jamaica," her
mother said.

156

Jamaica took the dog to her room. She could hear her mother say, "It probably belongs to a girl just like Jamaica."

After dessert Jamaica went to her room very quietly.

She held the dog up and looked at it closely.

Then she tossed it on a chair.

"Jamaica," her mother called from the kitchen.

"Have you forgotten? It's your turn to dry the dishes."

"Do I have to, Mother? I don't feel good," Jamaica answered.

Jamaica heard the pots rattle.

Then she heard her mother's steps.

Her mother came in quietly, sat down by Jamaica, and looked at the stuffed dog, which lay alone on the chair.

She didn't say anything.

After a while she put her arms around Jamaica and squeezed for a long time.

"Mother, I want to take the dog back to the park," Jamaica said.

"We'll go first thing in the morning." Her mother smiled.

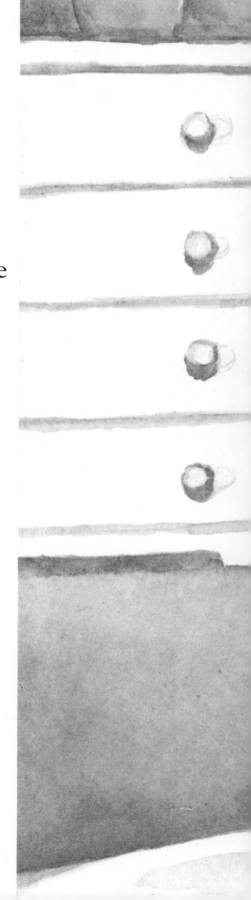

Jamaica ran to the park house and plopped the stuffed dog on the counter.

"I found this by the slide," she told the young man.

"Oh, hi. Aren't you the girl who gave me the hat last night?"

"Yes," said Jamaica, feeling hot around her ears.

"You sure do find a lot of things. I'll put it on the Lost and Found shelf."

Jamaica stood watching him.

"Is that all?" he asked. "You didn't find anything else, did you?"

"No. That's all." She stayed to watch him put the dog on a shelf behind him.

"I'm sure some little girl or boy will come in after it today, a nice little dog like that," the young man said.

Jamaica ran outside.

She didn't feel like playing alone.

There was no one else at the park but her mother, who sat on a bench.

Then Jamaica saw a girl and her mother cross the street to the park.

"Hi. I'm Jamaica. What's your name?" she said to the girl.

The girl let go of her mother's hand. "Kristin," she said.

"Do you want to climb the jungle gym with me, Kristin?" Jamaica said.

Kristin ran toward Jamaica. "Yes, but I have to find something first."

"What?" asked Jamaica. Kristin was bending under the slide.

"What did you lose?" said Jamaica.

"Edgar dog. I brought him with me yesterday and now I can't find him," Kristin answered.

"Was he kind of gray with black ears?" Jamaica couldn't keep from shouting. "Come along with me."

The young man in the park house looked over the counter at the two girls.

"Now what have you found?" he asked Jamaica.

But this time Jamaica didn't drop anything onto the counter.

Instead, she smiled her biggest smile. "I found the girl who belongs to that stuffed dog."

Jamaica was almost as happy as Kristin, who took Edgar dog in her arms and gave him a big welcome-back hug.

THINK IT OVER

1. What lesson did Jamaica learn?

2. How did you feel when Jamaica returned the dog?

WRITE

Imagine that you are Kristin. Write a thank-you note to Jamaica.

LOST AND FOUND

What do you think Jamaica would have done if she had found the bear?

· ·

What would you have done if you were the child in the stories?

· ·

WRITER'S WORKSHOP Pretend that Jamaica is lost and the boy from "Lost!" finds her. Write a play. Tell what the boy and girl would say.

CONNECTIONS

JO ANN JEONG

When Jo Ann Jeong was a girl, she visited a forest with her class. A park ranger told the children about the plants and animals there. Jo Ann thought to herself, "What a great job!"

Jo Ann Jeong never forgot that field trip. When she grew up, she became a park ranger for Golden Gate National Recreation Area in California.

■ Write about the job of a park ranger. Tell why this job might be fun.

170

A GREAT JOB FOR ME

Think of a time when you said to yourself, "What a great job!" What job would you like to have someday? On a sheet of paper, write about your dream job.

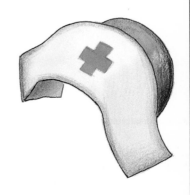

NATIONAL PARKS

Get a book about national parks from the library. What is special about each park? Which park would you like to see? Make a chart like this one with your classmates.

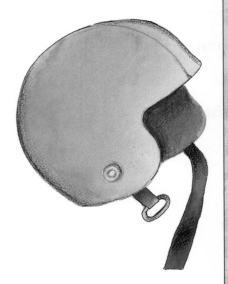

Name of Park	Where the Park Is	How It Is Special
Sequoia National Park	California	Huge trees

GLOSSARY

A

across   Travis and his dad sailed **across** the river.

again   Mark swam in the morning and **again** after lunch.

air   The wind blew cold **air** into the room.

almost   The sun was going down, so it was **almost** night.

alone   Leon was with me, so I was not **alone.**

also   Put on your socks and **also** your shoes.

animals   Cows and pigs are farm **animals.**

animals

B

because   I laughed at the joke **because** it was funny.

believe   Jan does not **believe** that ants can talk.

blue   Our flag is red, white, and **blue.**

books   I like to read **books** about birds.

books

C

city   There are many cars and people in a **city.**

clock   A **clock** shows us what time it is.

close   Rick lives so **close** to school that he can walk.

clock

D

dinner   My dad cooked **dinner** for us.

E

else   I want something **else** to eat.

enough   I am old **enough** to ride a bike.

eyes   You cannot see me with your **eyes** closed.

eyes

F

far   She hit the ball **far** up into the sky.

few   I have only a **few** pennies.

flower   The red **flower** grew by the tree.

found   Melinda lost her cat, but I **found** it.

fruit   Oranges and apples are **fruit.**

few

173

G

glows   The fire **glows** in the dark.

gone   Jeff has **gone** to the beach.

gray   The clouds were **gray** before it rained.

great   We had a **great** time on the boat.

growing   The baby is **growing** fast.

gray

H

head   You wear a hat on your **head.**

hear   Did you **hear** a dog bark?

himself   Joel can tie his shoes by **himself.**

hurt   Kim fell down and **hurt** her leg.

hurt

head

I

idea   Mario had the best **idea** for how to make a kite.

K

knew   Peter **knew** all about lions.

L

ladder   Mom stands on the **ladder** to paint the house.

later   Let's play now and pick up our toys **later.**

lay   I **lay** on the grass and looked up at the sky.

long   It took Rob a **long** time to walk home.

lay

M

matter   No **matter** how hard you try, you can't fly.

moon   The **moon** looked like a white ball in the sky.

moon

N

near   I stood **near** my mother and held her hand.

never   **Never** mind, I'll clean up the mess later.

near

O

or   We can play inside **or** we can play outside.

P

paper
paper   Tonya made a hat out of **paper.**

park   Trees and grass grow all over the **park.**

peace   Mom wants **peace** and quiet when she is sleeping.

people   Many **people** went to the show.

picture   I can draw a **picture** of a cow.

please   **Please** open the door for me.

pointing   The teacher was **pointing** to a word.

pretty   The flowers are very **pretty.**

picture

R

rain   Her bike got wet in the **rain.**

room   My toys and bed are in my **room.**

rain

room

S

scare   You will **scare** the baby with that toy.

school   We read and write at **school.**

seeds   Apple trees grow from apple **seeds.**

sky   From my window I can see the blue **sky.**

sky

sleep   At night we **sleep** in our beds.

sleeve   Put your arm in the **sleeve** of your coat.

smiled   Ben **smiled** because he was happy.

snow   We played outside in the **snow.**

star   I looked up and saw a **star** in the sky.

started   Rita opened the book and **started** to read.

stood   Jackie sat down, and then she **stood** up.

smile

story   The teacher read a **story** about a frog.

street   We saw the bus coming up the **street.**

such   We had **such** a good time swimming that we didn't want to stop.

sure   She **sure** can run fast!

surprise   It was a big **surprise** to get my own dog.

star

street

T

talk   I will **talk** to Terrence about his trip.

thought   Liz **thought** the game was silly.

threw   Bill **threw** the ball, and Sandy ran to catch it.

tired   Eric was so **tired** that he took a nap.

touch   I like to **touch** the cat's soft fur.

turning   The leaves were falling and **turning** in the wind.

tweet   **Tweet** is a sound that birds make.

talk

threw

turning

U

under   Our dog sleeps **under** my bed.

until   We will stay inside **until** the rain stops.

used   They **used** bricks to build a house.

under

W

while   We sat on the steps for a little **while.**

won't   Karen is sick, so she **won't** be at the party.